BEFORE YOU GET MARRIED

5 Power Questions to Ask Before Taking the Next Step

Volume 1

RAY MURRAY

IRM PUBLISHING

*To the One who knew me before I was formed in my mother's womb and
created the purpose for my life,
I offer my deepest gratitude.*

*God, I thank You for Your patience with me and for walking with me every
step of this journey to discovering my purpose. This book is the first
installment of my thank you.*

Acknowledgments

To my wife, Vicki: Thank you for your listening ear and your willingness to be an impromptu audience for my musings. Your love and support mean the world to me.

To our children, Corey, Patrice, Julian, Jayden, and Kenedi, and our grandson, CJ: This book is part of my gift of generational wealth to you. My prayer is that the wisdom shared in this book will impact your lives in some way and guide you on your own journeys. Let this be a reminder to walk with authority in your purpose and refuse to let go of your dreams.

To Jalon, Duke, and Omar: Our conversations helped confirm a part of God's plan for my life. This marriage literacy topic is needed and you all helped me to see that. Your friendship and insights have been invaluable.

To my brother, Pastor Jon Decuir: Thank you for being the constant encouragement and accountability that I needed to get here. You inspired me to write. This is just the beginning.

And finally to my parents Bishop Donald R. Murray and Lady Gwendolyn Murray I cannot thank you enough for your love and support throughout my life. I have always wanted you to look at my life and be confident that it was worth all the sacrifices. Thank you for it all.

Introduction

As you make the rounds announcing your engagement…

all you hear is, "Congratulations!" Everyone is excited about the dress, the venue, and the honeymoon. But when marriages start to fall apart, suddenly everyone has all the questions. Questions that could have been asked before the wedding. Why is that?

For over a decade as a pastor, counselor and relationship coach, I have worked with countless couples from all walks of life. And I have noticed a pattern: many couples step into marriage unprepared for the realities that lie ahead. Why? Because they were caught up in the excitement of the moment. They focused on the thrill of getting married, the romance of the honeymoon, and the joy of starting a new life together, but they did not take the time to ask the questions that really matter. They did not dig deep enough.

Marriage is beautiful, but it is also serious. It is easily one of the top three decisions you will ever make in your life. It is too important to go into without a clear understanding of your partner, your relationship, and the life you are committing to build together. I am passionate about this because I have seen how asking the right questions, honest and courageous questions, can transform relationships and save people from unnecessary heartache.

I know people often say, "You do not know what you do not know." But what if you could know more? What if you could avoid the blind spots that derail so many marriages simply by being intentional about the conversations you have before you say, "I do"? What if you could start your marriage with clarity, confidence, and alignment instead of figuring it all out the hard way later?

This book is here to help you do just that. Whether you are newly engaged, seriously dating, or trying to figure out if your partner is "the one," Before You Get Married: 5 Power Questions to Ask Before Taking the Next Step will give you practical tools to build a marriage that thrives. These are the kinds of questions that challenge you, stretch you, and deepen your understanding of each other and your future together.

Marriage is not just about the wedding or the honeymoon. It's about building a life that lasts. You don't need to wait for cracks to show before asking the important questions. By the time you finish this book and engage with the workbook, you will gain the tools to create a strong foundation for a marriage grounded in purpose, mutual understanding, and true partnership.

Your future together starts now. Let's get to work.

Chapter 1
What's Your Vision?

"The only thing worse than being blind is having sight but no vision." [1]

- Helen Keller

Marriage is a journey that requires lots of prayer, careful thought, and intentional conversations. One of the most important conversations a couple needs to have before marriage is to discuss their vision. Do you know how many couples I encounter who have not had an in-depth series of conversations regarding a collective vision for their marriage? It's a setup for disaster.

There's a bible verse in Proverbs 29:18 that reads, "Where there is no vision, the people perish:"[2] Without vision, in the context of a relationship, there is nothing for a couple to use as a compass to guide their behavior, decisions, or efforts. Honestly, most of the couples I've counseled with marriage issues—ranging from manageable to daunting—never thought to discuss vision. They had no idea how critical it was, but now they understand. And let me be clear: this is not a generic, "all couples should want this kind of marriage" vision. I'm talking about a vision specifically tailored to the relationship between the two people in the relationship. Sitting down with your partner and asking, "What's our vision?" presents a powerful opportunity to define the purpose of the marriage in a customized way. A series of conversations focused on this question also allows each individual to find a point of understanding regarding the role that each of them will play in the future success of the union. Without question, having a lasting and healthy relationship at every stage of your life requires a defined vision. So, in this chapter, we'll discuss the importance of having a shared vision for yourself and your marriage and how to create one.

Why is Vision So Important?

Vision is everything. If you can't see it, you'll never reach it. I know that sounds corny, but I can explain it best with an illustration. I want you to imagine that I just dumped 1825 pieces of a puzzle on a table in front of you and your partner. No box, just pieces. I give the instructions that you can take only one of those tiny pieces each day to start solving the puzzle. On day 1, you choose a piece together to lay out; on day 2, you select another piece from the now 1824 piece pile to try to fit with the piece from the day before, and so on. You can only pick one piece per day. Before leaving, I tell you, "Oh, by the way, you won't have access to the box; your love for each other should be enough to make sense of the puzzle." Of course, the box I'm talking about is the one the manufacturer sent with a "finished" picture of the puzzle on the cover.

Can you imagine how frustrated the two of you would be? After discussing how ridiculous this challenge was, one of you would eventually say, "And what does love have to do with solving this puzzle when we have no picture to go by?!" Oh, and one more thing, did I say there was a million dollars on the line? That would be the only feasible incentive motivating you to at least try to complete this impossible challenge. And while the money would ensure that you would at least try, eventually, you would quit because you had no picture. Because when it comes to finishing a puzzle, I don't care how much you love each other and how much money is on the line; if you don't have the "finished" picture of the puzzle, it's impossible to solve. Why? You'd have no idea how to start and no way of knowing each day if you were even heading in the right direction. You'd be living every day trying to make sense of it without direction. That's the frustration of living without vision.

. . .

Vision is the box the puzzle pieces came in with the finished product printed on the cover. Vision is the picture of what it should look like at the end. It drives you every day because you have a tool to measure progress and direction. Without it, you would never know if you were even close. That's how critical vision is.

I chose 1825 pieces for a specific and sobering reason. 1825 is the number of days in 5 years. Can you imagine trying to solve this puzzle for five years with no picture? Could this be a contributing factor to the reason that 20% of marriages end in divorce in the first five years?[3] How many of these couples tried to make sense of each day without a picture to go by? Imagine the frustration of a couple trying to make sense of marriage without a vision.

Why is vision so important? Because it answers the question, "What should this look like at the end?" It is a decisive moment of clarity where you define what the end looks like before the beginning. This is where the beauty of hope and faith meet up! Vision, when it is present, provides an environment in which the hope for your marriage and the faith to work on it intersect.

Now, let's drill down a little further. Vision is important because, for a couple, it answers the question "when we look back on our lives together, what do we want to have accomplished?" When you can answer that, the vision determines whether you're getting closer to it or farther away. With this mindset, each day becomes a piece of the picture. A clear vision provides a helpful reference for making sense of each day, ensuring your choices align with the shared picture you've agreed upon. That's why vision is critical; it's like the puzzle box picture that guides how you put it all together.

The illustration of the picture on the puzzle box resonates with me because it was a God-given revelation right when I needed it in my marriage. We had hit a point where it became clear we needed fundamental change, and I realized my wife and I were missing a clear vision for our marriage. I had completely missed it because I had never applied the impact of vision on anything other than an individual or work context. I'll explain.

The power of a well-defined vision brings clarity to every day and, subsequently, years to come. For most of you reading this book, this is not your first time hearing about the power of vision for an individual. However, most people take a leap from individuals to companies when it comes to vision. Individuals and companies have visions, but what about couples, friends, and even families? You see, any partnership that exists needs a vision. Ultimately, what's the point of being in any long-lasting relationship if there's no vision for its growth, evolution, and impact? That same realization hit me regarding my closest friends. Now, we meet to talk about our individual and collective visions, asking questions like, "Who do we want to be as a group in 5, 10, or 15 years?" and "How will we rely on each other for support and resources in our personal and shared pursuits?" The same applies to you and your partner. Why are you together? What is the purpose and plan for your union? Why are the two of you together and not with someone else? What does God see in this? Be intentional about having these discussions before you get married because you want to know that your visions align. It's critical to be clear about your vision first and then come together to align on a shared vision as you step into the most significant partnership of your lives.

This vision concept has two critical parts before marriage. First, you need to establish your vision, and only then can you start discussing your shared vision as a couple. You can approach both steps with a similar strategy. So, let's explore that.

Defining My Vision In Three Words

When we think about defining vision, we often focus on goals such as getting married (the event, not the life you build afterward), buying a home, achieving six-figure salaries, or launching seven-figure businesses. But vision goes beyond these milestones; it's about creating a deeper context for who you are becoming. I learned this strategy from Jean-Marie Jobs, an incredible leader and coach, who challenged me to expand my definition of vision. She described vision not just as what you do but as who you are, a way of being that leaves a lasting impact on the world. Think about that. Can you see how that shift in perspective can be so powerful? Yes, goals are still a part of the journey, but they don't have to define the entire vision. Vision can transcend the limits of any single goal.

Now, what if your vision could surpass just achieving goals? What if vision didn't stop at a goal, leaving you wondering, "What's next?" after each milestone? You get married, then what? You hit six figures, then what? And here's a hard truth: if you don't hit these goals in the expected timeframe, does that mean you've failed in your vision? I can't tell you how many people I know who've hit their goals and are still dissatisfied with their lives. Don't get me wrong, goals are essential, and your efforts to reach them matter. But what if there's more?

Remember, the journey is just as important as the destination. How you get there matters, and the person you become along the way matters even more. What if your vision wasn't just about what you achieve but about who you are becoming? What if I told you there's a way to walk in your vision while achieving your goals? What you do may end, but who you are becoming has no limits. Let me share an example.

I've narrowed my vision down to three words. These words come from an exercise where I listed all the characteristics that identify who God created me to be—words like inspiration, teacher, and connector. I chose my top three from that list: freedom, authenticity, and wisdom. These three words capture my most impactful characteristics and represent the greatest gifts I offer to the world. When people are around me, they experience freedom, authenticity, and wisdom. When I walk in these words, I'm at my best, and my impact is at its greatest. Every morning, in my prayer time, I remind myself that God has given me freedom, authenticity, and wisdom to inspire this generation. That's my vision.

Of course, some days are more difficult than others to live out this vision, but when I do, my "being" impacts my "doing." As I pursue my goals, I also enjoy the fruits of the journey because I'm living out my vision along the way. It's like planting a garden, you get back what you plant. So ask yourself, what harvest do you want to experience? What do you want to grow in your life that will impact you and those around you?

. . .

My greatest joy is knowing that people leave my presence feeling "free," lighter than they did when we first connected, more joyful, and inspired. Whether after a speech, a class, or even a conversation, when people say they felt my authenticity or were moved by my honesty, I know I'm living my vision. And I want the same for you. We'll dive into the "These Three Words" exercise at the end of this chapter, but as you read through the next set of questions, start reflecting on your own words. Go ahead and read them, but hold off on answering for now and let me first explain why this is so crucial.

"These Three Words" Questions:

• **What are my characteristics?**

(Inspiring, Caring, Loyal, etc.)

• **What matters most to me?**

(freedom, integrity, authenticity, etc.)

• **What gifts do I believe God gave me to leave with the world?**

(wisdom, love, joy, etc.)

From all the words now written on the page, what three words best capture the heart of who you are?

* * *

If you have trouble with the questions above...
Start by discussing the following questions with your partner to arrive at the answer for your "three words" question.

Ask your partner to answer these questions about you and discuss:

• **From your perspective, what are my values?**

(compassion, generosity, innovation, etc)

• **From what you've observed, what are my core beliefs and principles?**

(honesty, respect, leadership, kindness, etc.)

• From what you've experienced, how do I impact people when they are in my presence?
(loved, supported, empowered, inspired, etc.)

Note: During this process, your partner is giving you feedback that can give you another perspective on yourself. This exercise will provide more clarity as you condense this discussion into your **three-word vision**.

Defining Our Vision in Three Words

After completing this exercise individually, revisit the conversation as a couple. This time, focus on the questions through the lens of lifelong partnership. While the process follows a similar path to the individual exercise, it shifts toward the shared journey of your relationship. Use the following questions to guide your discussion:

• What are your characteristics as a couple?
(Write as many as you can.)

• What gift do you believe God gave you, as a couple, to leave with each other in the relationship?

(In other words, at the end of your lives, how would you want your spouse to say they experienced your love?)

• **What words describe the gift you want others to receive when they are with the two of you?**
(Another way to ask this is: What do you want others to see or experience as a result of your presence together?)

From all the words now written on the page, what three words best capture the heart of who you are as a couple?

* * *

If you have trouble with the questions above, start by discussing the following questions to arrive at the answer for your "These Three Words" questions.

Discuss these questions about the two of you as a couple:

• What are OUR values as a couple?
• What are OUR core beliefs and principles?
• In what ways do WE want to leave our mark on the world?

Note: Please avoid answering these questions with material goals or achievements in mind. Instead, focus on the impact you want your presence to have on others. For example, instead of saying, "We need to make a million dollars to help people," consider the word "generosity." Your financial success might be one way to express generosity, but it's not the only way.

"These Three Words" In Real Life...

Let's see how the three-word vision plays out in a real-life example.

During one of my counseling sessions with an engaged couple, I introduced them to this exercise, and they identified their three words: sacrifice, intentionality, and transparency. Their vision for their relationship was focused on "sacrifice," where they would prioritize loving each other sacrificially. They envisioned "intentionality" in their partnership, ensuring they would celebrate, affirm, and carve out meaningful time for each other. This was their strategy to uphold honor and respect as their foundation. Lastly, they committed to "transparency," a commitment to be consistently open and honest through the highs and lows of their journey together.

Can you imagine the depth of love they will create by pursuing this vision? Now, think about their relationship's ripple effect on those around them, the people who will witness a couple living out this vision. The impact naturally extends beyond them, touching everyone they encounter. Planting these seeds daily creates a garden of beauty and lasting legacy.

Of course, this doesn't mean every day will be perfect; they're human, and grace is necessary. But the hope is that, as a couple, they remain committed to the daily pursuit of their vision. For this couple, sacrifice, intentionality, and transparency create the picture on their puzzle box, and each day is a piece of that puzzle. Now, they have a clear vision to guide how the pieces fit together, shaping the marriage and partnership they've envisioned. And when things drift (and they will), they have a vision to get them back on track.

Conclusion

Please remember that vision can only become a reality with repetition. When we refer to your vision as an individual or a couple, we're also discussing the idea of identity (who you are as an individual or a couple). And identity is not established in one day. You don't know your name because someone called you by your name once. It was a daily engagement until you started to respond to it. And now, no one can make you second guess your name. Vision works the same way. These three words must be discussed and practiced often. As you take this journey together, create an atmosphere that allows you to hold each other accountable to the vision. Talk about it weekly so that you have an unshakable grasp on your vision over time.

The concept of vision is not just for businesses or individuals; it is also critical for couples. A clear vision of a successful lifelong partnership is valuable in creating a fulfilling and satisfying union. You need a clear vision to give your relationship the best possible chance for success. Without it, what will guide you? How will you measure the health of your relationship? Let's take it further: vision and purpose are inseparable. Without vision, there's no purpose—meaning you lose your "why." And, to have a real shot at this, you need to know why you're in it. Vision is what inspires you when your partner can't. It's what keeps you accountable when you feel like coasting. Vision reminds you that tomorrow requires realignment with the picture you've set because today's actions didn't quite fit. Vision is essential because the image on the front of the puzzle box shows you the finished product before you start.

So, before you go any further, stop now and have the necessary conversations around the question, "What's your vision?" It will provide clarity and purpose for your relationship in ways you didn't even know you needed. Trust me, your future will thank you. This chapter is for your future.

"Your vision will become clear only when you can look into your own heart. Who looks outside, dreams; who looks inside, awakes."

4

- Carl Jung

REFLECTION QUESTIONS

1.Have you taken the time to define what success in marriage looks like for you and how it aligns with your partner's vision?

2.Do you know the three words that capture the essence of who you are and how they shape your partnership?

3.Imagine having a clear, actionable sentence that sums up your personal and shared vision; how would that guide your decisions daily?

4.Are you confident you've explored the values and principles that form the foundation of your relationship?

5.What difference would it make to have a tool that ensures you and your partner are building toward the same vision with clarity and purpose?

YOUR NEXT STEP ...

Your vision is the foundation of your relationship, shaping how you grow together and what you ultimately build as a couple. While reflecting on these questions is a great start, creating a clear, actionable vision requires more than just thoughts; it demands intentional work. The exercises in the workbook will guide you step-by-step, helping you define and refine your vision.

Chapter 2

Is Your Partner Compatible With Your Purpose?

"The two most important days in your life are the day you are born and the day you find out why."[1]

— *Mark Twain*

In my conversations with couples at different stages of their relationships, I've noticed that many enter into exclusive relationships without asking if their life purposes are genuinely compatible. Simply put, they overlook the critical question of whether their partner aligns with the purpose for which God created them. I want you to take a moment to think about this sobering reality. Without consideration, you could be in a relationship with someone that creates conflict with the reason for your existence (it happens more often than you know). Sure, it's nice that you both enjoy similar things like walks on the beach, pizza, and 90s R&B

(which, by the way, is the absolute best, in my opinion). But those common interests won't sustain you when facing life's challenges with a partner who doesn't support the person you are truly meant to be. You can navigate the challenges of not sharing the same hobbies more quickly than being incompatible with your partner's purpose.

Purpose incompatibility can lead to all sorts of issues in the long run, such as dissatisfaction, unfulfillment, resentment, and immense frustration stemming from the inability to share your true self with your partner. Even when neither partner intends to create conflict, I've often seen couples locked in some intense struggles because one person feels lost trying to find their place in the life of a partner with a clear sense of purpose. And that's only one part of the pain. On the other side is the partner who feels overlooked, as their partner's purpose seems to take priority, constantly competing with what feels like the object of your partner's affection. Or even worse, when a partner doesn't understand or see the value in their partner's purpose.

Thankfully, you can prevent many of these problems by having purposeful discussions. This discussion starts with the question, "Are they compatible with my purpose?" In the context of life-long commitment, there is so much more to life than enjoying movies or sharing common interests (don't get me wrong, all of that is great in context). Still, it's about going deeper and discovering if you and your partner align regarding your life's purpose. This chapter will explore why purpose compatibility is critical and provide valuable insights into navigating these conversations effectively.

What is Purpose?

Before we get into why your partner's compatibility with your purpose is essential, let's first understand what we mean by "purpose." Your purpose is the reason why you exist. It gives your life meaning because it details how God determined you would impact the world. Once you discover it, it's the driving force behind everything you do and the core of what you hope to be and achieve during your time on Earth. Pablo Picasso said, "The meaning of life is finding your gift. The purpose of life is to give it away."[2]

Everyone's purpose in life is shaped by a beautiful mix of their passions, values, and aspirations. For some people, their purpose is connected to their work. As their career takes shape and they experience fulfillment, it becomes a way to express themselves, grow personally, and leave a positive mark in their field. They are motivated to excel, contribute to their chosen industry, and leave a lasting legacy.

. . .

Others discover their purpose in their relationships, family, or serving their community. They come alive when nurturing and supporting others and ensuring they thrive. Their purpose lies in creating strong bonds, fostering a loving and supportive environment, and making a positive difference in the lives of the people they care about. They find meaning in the relationships they build and their impact on the people they engage with.

Others find purpose in their deep desire to improve the world, driven by the need to address social, environmental, or humanitarian issues. Their purpose is to create positive change, fight for justice and equality, and contribute to the well-being of humanity. They want to leave a lasting impact and a legacy beyond their lifetime.

At the core, everyone's purpose reflects who they are and what they genuinely believe in. Whether centered around their career or family or making a difference in the world, purpose, at its best, is the driving force that fuels passion and shapes decisions. When we embrace and actively pursue our purpose, we tap into a more profound sense of fulfillment, aligning our lives with what truly resonates with our values and dreams.

Understanding and aligning our purpose is vital, especially regarding our relationships. When individuals enter a partnership without considering if their purposes are compatible, the chances of encountering difficulties in the future are great. Conflicts can arise without a shared understanding of purpose or recognition of each other's purposes, and the relationship can become distant or even unsatisfying.

When Purpose has no Partner

Imagine a couple where one partner is deeply passionate about their career and dedicated to significantly impacting their field, even if it means long hours and less time at home. In contrast, the other partner finds purpose in nurturing a strong, thriving family, valuing time spent at home, and seeing work primarily as a way to support that lifestyle. Picture those conversations. Chances are you've witnessed a few or at least heard about them. Imagine the tension that builds when one partner sees their purpose in career success while the other believes their purpose is rooted in family life. If they are deeply connected to their purpose but confused by the purpose of their mate, it leads to inevitable conflict. Because purpose often determines the focus. With purpose compatibility, supporting and comprehending each other's priorities and aspirations can be more manageable. When purpose compatibility is not present, it can result in emotions of bitterness, unrealized hopes, and an increasing emotional distance between two people. Why? Because every purpose comes with its own set of demands, and when those demands clash, the couple may end up on two separate islands with no bridge to connect them.

When Purpose Has a Partner

On the other hand, imagine a couple that has purpose compatibility. When this type of compatibility is present, it strengthens the bond between the two, creating a solid foundation for fulfillment and harmony. Purpose compatibility means individuals understand and value each other's life goals, values, and aspirations. They don't have to be the same or even in the same field, but they wholeheartedly support each other's purposes while finding common ground and shared objectives. They become each other's biggest supporters, offering encouragement and guidance as they strive towards their personal and joint aspirations. Each one holds space for the demands of their partner's purpose.

Imagine a couple where one partner is a lawyer committed to providing legal services to underserved communities. At the same time, the other is an entrepreneur passionate about building successful businesses to give back to those same communities. Both have demanding careers that require long hours, but their purposes align with helping others in different ways. The entrepreneur could eventually reach a level of success that enables them to fund the lawyer's pro-bono cases while the lawyer takes care of the entrepreneur's legal demands. That's purpose compatibility, their individual goals complement each other without causing conflict, allowing them to fully support one another without resentment or dissatisfaction.

In a relationship characterized by purpose compatibility, partners embark on individual journeys and find ways to create a shared vision and purpose. It energizes them to see their partner thriving in their pursuit of purpose, and they never see their passion for their purpose as a threat. They find ways to align their paths, utilizing their unique strengths and aspirations to complement each other. These partners become teammates, supporting each other as they navigate the ups and downs of life. This shared purpose becomes a source of motivation, inspiration, and a deeper connection within the relationship.

Other Ways that Purpose Compatibility Enhances a Marriage

You'll experience a more satisfying relationship

When you're with someone who compliments your purpose, you'll know. Your connection and understanding will grow deeper over time, leading to a meaningful and fulfilling relationship built on a shared purpose and common objectives. This alignment of values and goals allows you to support and uplift each other, fostering a sense of unity and collaboration.

You'll Be More Motivated to Achieve Your Goals

You'll feel more motivated to work towards your goals when you're in a relationship with someone who supports and encourages your purpose. Your partner can be a source of inspiration and accountability, helping you stay focused on fighting through the obstacles to completion. When your partner supports and encourages your purpose, their belief in you can light a fire within you to pursue your goals. They can provide valuable guidance, offer constructive feedback, and celebrate your successes, creating a dynamic of mutual growth and support in your relationship.

In Real Life...

Earlier in the section titled "When Purpose Has a Partner," we saw the power of purpose compatibility. Now, let's look at a real-life example to illustrate what happens when the couple realizes they are not compatible with their partner's purpose.

. . .

Example: The Investment Banker and the Artist

Ryan is an investment banker passionate about building wealth for himself and his clients. His life's motivation is to make a difference in the world through his work.

Tiana is an artist passionate about expressing herself through her art. She's always been drawn to the creative process and sees her work as a way to connect with others and inspire them.

When Ryan and Tiana first met, they were immediately attracted to each other's passion and energy. They started dating and quickly fell in love, but over time, they realized something was off. Ryan continued building his investment portfolio and creating wealth while growing frustrated with Tiana's lack of excitement and support for his wealth and financial expansion. The issue was more severe than they knew. Tiana never told Ryan that before him, she always thought of people who were into making a lot of money as shallow and greedy. How could that be his purpose when it seemed so selfish? She loved Ryan but hated to talk about his financial exploits. And the long hours he kept at work seemed pointless, just to make more money. It didn't make sense to her, and Ryan could feel that. The more he spoke about his business ventures, the more distant Tiana became.

.   .   .

Tiana felt the same energy from Ryan. She was so passionate about her art and creative pursuits. But, when she would talk about her new projects with Ryan, he was not interested. He believed that creative pursuits, like art, were hobbies, not a life purpose. In all honesty, he was trying to wait her out. He figured if he focused on being there for her long enough, she would eventually grow out of it, but she never did.

While they loved each other, they realized they had no connection to each other's purpose. They had never talked about purpose. Initially, it didn't seem that it would ever get in the way. They each had a purpose, and that seemed to be enough. But when their true feelings surrounding each other's purpose came to the surface, they realized it did matter. They loved going out to dinner and spending time together, but when they got to dinner, they couldn't talk about their day because neither was genuinely interested in their partner's journey.

Eventually, they decided to end their relationship, realizing they were incompatible with each other's purpose. While they still respected and cared for each other, they knew they needed to find partners who understood and supported their purpose.

.   .   .

Question: What would have happened if they had decided to have this conversation early on in their relationship instead of living through painful years and conflicting feelings before being forced to address it? Can you see how much time they would've saved if they had known how important it was to investigate this question?

Purpose compatibility matters.

The fact that their purposes seemed so different was not critical to their relationship failure. The lack of compatibility had more to do with what they believed about the purpose of their partner. Neither partner could see the value in the purpose of the other, which led to the truth of the incompatibility.

As you can see, your purpose doesn't have to be in the same industry as your partner. What matters most is what you believe about their purpose. Is it something you find value in? Can you hold space for the demands of their purpose? Do you believe in it and them? Asking these questions helps you to assess purpose compatibility. And yes, it matters.

Conclusion

Discussing your partner's compatibility with your purpose is vital for a successful and fulfilling relationship. When you find a partner who shares your values and goals, you'll develop a deep and meaningful connection strengthened by working together to achieve your respective purposes.

Adding purpose compatibility to the list of areas to explore before marriage might seem exhausting as you add another obstacle to your vision of a lifelong partner, but trust me; you don't want to say I do before considering this critical question. Who you are as an individual is as important as your life with your partner. You and your partner were individuals before you were together. Honor yourself by reflecting on your purpose and seeking a partner who appreciates it. When you are intentional about your life in this way, you set the foundation for a fulfilling relationship that supports you in pursuing your life's purpose.

Remember, honest and open communication will help you determine purpose compatibility. Engage in intentional conversations about individual purposes, explore values, and find common ground. Practice active listening, empathy, and a genuine curiosity to understand each other's motivations and aspirations. By creating a supportive, trusting, and under-standing environment, couples can strengthen purpose compatibility, fostering a relationship that thrives on shared vision and mutual growth.

REFLECTION QUESTIONS

1. Have you fully explored your life's purpose and how it connects or conflicts with your partner's?

2. Do you know how your partner's purpose complements or challenges your own and what that means for your future?

3. What would change if you had a step-by-step process to define your purpose, evaluate compatibility, and set healthy boundaries?

4. When was the last time you had an intentional conversation about how your individual purposes align as a couple?

5. How much would it mean to your future to uncover potential red flags, or to confirm your compatibility, before you take the next step?

YOUR NEXT STEP ...

Purpose is the heartbeat of who you are, and finding alignment with your partner is one of the most critical aspects of building a lasting relationship. These reflections help you begin to explore this alignment, but the real transformation happens when you take the time to work through the deeper questions. The workbook provides a structured approach to uncovering your purpose, assessing compatibility, and having the conversations that matter most. Let this be the step that ensures your partner not only loves who you are but supports where you're going.

Chapter 3
Can We Talk About Finances?

"Honesty is the first chapter in the book of wisdom."[1]
- Thomas Jefferson

Discussing money can be a touchy subject in any relationship. Many couples tend to avoid conversations about their finances because they worry it might lead to arguments or uncover embarrassing parts of their financial situation. Let's be honest: in everyday life, this is one of the most challenging conversations you can have with your partner. However, avoiding these financial conversations can create significant issues in the future.

But let's not look down the road just yet. What about the present state of your relationship? Refusing to talk about money can chip away at trust from the beginning. If you intentionally keep your partner in the dark about your financial situation, you're holding back. And as time goes on, avoiding this tough conversation only widens the gap in your relationship. A strong relationship is built on trust and vulnerability, and hiding your finances won't create the openness your relationship needs to thrive.

If you want a relationship built on trust, you have to choose courage and walk through this conversation, sharing the truth of your finances with your partner. In this chapter, we'll dive into why it's so important to be honest and build financial trust in relationships. We'll also provide real-life examples and stories to help you better understand these concepts.

Let's Give You Some Context

By now, most people know that "money situations," as I call them, can cause a lot of stress in relationships. The loss of a job, student debt, and overspending are all events that can lead to significant tension. But we often overlook the mismanaged conversations and behaviors that lead to these "money situations." Just talking about money can cause high levels of anxiety for a couple, leading to actions that start to erode the relationship.

To help you understand the impact of these conversations, let's consider these statistics:

- According to a study by Ramsey Solutions, money fights are the second leading cause of divorce, following infidelity.[2]
- A survey conducted by MagnifyMoney found that 21% of couples reported hiding a purchase of $500 or more from their partner.[3]
- According to a survey by Ally Bank, 70% of couples argued about money more than any other topic.[4]

The toxicity of mismanaging finances in a relationship can cause ongoing arguments, deceit, and, at its worst, divorce. But the good news is that it doesn't have to be this way. Imagine how relationships would flourish if couples committed to financial honesty and integrity. By openly discussing their financial situations, they could establish a solid foundation of trust and mutual respect that touches every area of their relationship. If you can talk about finances, you can talk about almost anything.

Honesty is the Best Policy

In long-term relationships, being open with your partner about your financial situation is critical for creating a healthy foundation. This means having candid discussions about debts, income, spending habits, and financial goals. Transparency helps avoid misunderstandings and allows you to make well-informed decisions together.

I understand that taking this step in your relationship requires courage. Discussing finances is deeply personal, especially as you approach marriage, because it reveals so much about your values and your approach to money. And let's be honest, in our culture, money is often tied to identity. Whether you have it, don't have it, or how you handle it, money can shape your sense of worth.

When your thoughts about money or the opinions of others are mismanaged, it can lead to feelings of inadequacy or even shame. These conversations aren't just about numbers; they touch on who you are and how you view yourself in the world. You deserve to know if your partner can truly accept all of you: the good, the bad, and the ugly.

Financial Surprises: A Real-Life Example

Imagine you and your partner are considering buying a new home. You've avoided the "finance" conversation because there's some debt you haven't disclosed. When the truth finally comes out, it's during a meeting with your loan officer, who delivers the news for the first time. Suddenly, the house you both love and thought you could afford becomes unattainable due to the truth about your financial state.

This untimely surprise could lead to disappointment, anger, and resentment. I understand that having a challenging financial past can bring up feelings of humiliation or embarrassment. However, there's nothing more courageous in a relationship than allowing your partner to embrace all of you and support you in an area of need.

The freedom of "baring it all" can only be topped by the joy of witnessing a partner's commitment to journey with you toward financial well-being. And let's not pretend that every situation will end like a tear-jerking 90s romantic comedy. Sometimes, a partner's reaction to the truth will not be pleasant. Either way, in those conversations, you must prepare to honor your partner's capacity to handle your financial reality.

The Rules of Engagement

When it's time to talk about finances, approach it with purpose. Preparing to "open up the books," as I call it, shouldn't be a casual conversation. It requires careful planning. So, as you get ready for this discussion, here are some guidelines to keep in mind.

. . .

Introduce the topic in a neutral way that reflects its importance.

For example: "Hey [insert name], as we're starting to talk about marriage, I think it's important for us to discuss where we are financially. Let's set aside some time to go over our finances, including things like debt, income, and future goals. That way, we can support each other and build together. What day works best for you to start this discussion?"

When you open up this discussion, be intentional with your tone. Avoid bringing up the topic during an argument or emotional moment, as this can lead to defensiveness.

Mentally prepare to contribute to a safe environment.

Prepare to refrain from being judgmental or reactive. Sit relaxed, and even if something surprises you, do your best to remain calm and ACTIVELY LISTEN before responding. If you tend to interrupt, have a journal nearby to jot down thoughts or questions instead of interrupting your partner.

Start with transparency, and
avoid justifying your situation.

When sharing your financial status, don't try to explain or rationalize decisions. Simply present the facts, including income, debt, and obligations.

Listen and ask clarifying questions.

After your partner shares their financial truth, focus on listening attentively as you ask thoughtful questions to better understand their financial history, goals and dreams. Foster a safe and open environment where dialogue can flow freely and support can thrive. You will take turns sharing during this conversation.

Part 2: "How Do We Build Financially?"

Now that you've shared your financial truths, shift the focus to building a financial future together. Ask each other these key questions:

- Who do we want to be financially? What are our goals and dreams as a couple?
- What steps do we need to take to accomplish these goals?
- How will we hold each other accountable for these steps?
- How will we handle disagreements on major financial decisions?

Conclusion

Talking about finances is challenging. Many couples avoid these conversations, hoping to avoid tension or embarrassment. But avoidance doesn't help the situation, it simply creates deeper issues down the road. Tackling finances head-on builds trust, transparency, and intimacy in your relationship

Remember, this process will require courage, grace, and empathy. Start in a neutral environment, share with honesty, and embrace the vulnerability of financial transparency. Ultimately, these conversations aren't just about money; they're about creating a relationship built on transparency, where trust can flourish.

REFLECTION QUESTIONS

1. Have you had the honest, transparent money conversations that are essential for building trust in your relationship?

2. Have you and your partner clearly defined your short-term, medium-term, and long-term financial goals?

3. How would it feel to have a step-by-step budgeting exercise to simplify your financial planning as a couple?

4. Are you confident in your understanding of your current financial situation, and do you have a plan to manage it together?

YOUR NEXT STEP ...

Money can be one of the greatest challenges or greatest strengths in your relationship, depending on how you approach it. These reflections provide a first step toward financial clarity, but lasting trust and alignment come from doing the work.

The workbook doesn't just ask questions; it equips you with exercises to define goals, create a budget, and develop habits that set you up for success. Don't let money become a source of division; use the workbook to build a financial foundation that strengthens your partnership.

Chapter 4
Who Breaks the Tie?

"In marriage, it's less about thinking alike and more about thinking together."[1]

-Anonymous

Marriage is a beautiful yet complex union, bringing together two people with unique backgrounds, beliefs, and life experiences. No matter how compatible you are, this reality remains. A marriage isn't just about the love you share; it's a partnership that thrives on compromise, empathy, and a commitment to working together as a team. But what happens when a couple disagrees on a significant issue and can't seem to reach a compromise? Do you just keep digging in your heels in a tug-of-war, trying to pull the other to your side? Or is there another alternative?

. . .

Think about the imagery of a tug-of-war between you and your partner. A tug-of-war is a competition that requires the participants to intentionally and forcefully use all the strength available to physically and mentally break down their opponent to submit to their will. Is this really how you want to treat the one you love? Unfortunately, this is the decision-making method used in relationships far too often. The exhaustion and pain a tug-of-war causes can damage you and your partner in ways that take years to repair, all because no one thought to decide how to decide.

I've counseled couples who've experienced deep struggles in their relationships because they couldn't find a way past the tug-of-war in their decision-making. If I'm being honest, I've felt that same pain in my own relationships as I focused more on being right than finding a solution. Choosing the "I'd rather be right" path too often leads to anger and lasting resentment at best, and at worst, it can cause irreversible damage that ends the relationship. No matter how it ends, your relationship suffers the loss of weeks, months, or even years of being unable to move forward in areas that significantly affect its health, growth, and maturity.

As a couple, you're going to face moments where you just disagree. It's a natural part of any committed relationship. But

I'm talking about those extreme times when you're on completely opposite sides of an issue, where compromise feels impossible, and one of you has to make the final call. This is where the idea of "breaking the tie" comes into play.

In this chapter, we will define this method and explore the importance of deciding who breaks the tie in decisive moments. We'll also discuss why this decision shouldn't be taken lightly and share examples of how this method can strengthen your relationship.

What Does It Mean to Break the Tie?

Breaking the tie is a method of decision-making that couples can use when they can't seem to agree on the path forward. It's an agreement between partners to designate one person who will "break the tie" if they cannot reach a decision together. This understanding allows the couple to identify the partner with the final say on a particular matter.

Simply put, deciding who breaks the tie means choosing which partner will take the lead. This is a big decision, and it's worth taking the time to understand the responsibility it entails. Leading in your relationship, no matter the topic, is an honor and should be handled with care.

"Leadership is not about being in charge. It's about taking care of those in your charge." [2]
— *Simon Sinek*

When I heard these words from Simon Sinek, I vowed never to forget them. They gave me a fresh perspective on the responsibility of leadership. True leadership is not about wielding authority or abusing power; it's about making decisions with a full understanding of the responsibility it entails. Whether in the public sphere or within the privacy of a marriage, authentic leadership prioritizes care and trust.

In a marriage, an authentic leader says, "The decision I make will greatly impact my partner. I'll be thoughtful, wise, and empathetic to the fact that this may not be how they see it, and yet I am honored that they trust me to make the final decision. Because they've given me this responsibility, I want them to feel cared for and heard, even when we don't agree." When the one who breaks the tie approaches their role with this mindset, trust can thrive even in moments of disagreement.

In the book of Genesis, God grants both man and woman dominion, emphasizing shared leadership responsibilities. While leadership may look different at times, both partners are called to lead with maturity and care. This shared responsibility ensures that decisions are made with honor and build trust.

Reasons Why Deciding Who Breaks the Tie Is Important

It prevents resentment.

Resentment is one of the most destructive emotions in a marriage. When one partner feels their voice isn't heard or their opinions don't matter, bitterness and anger can set in. The "who breaks the tie" method prevents this by ensuring both partners have a voice in the decision-making process. Feeling seen and heard goes a long way in protecting your relationship from resentment.

It promotes communication.

Discussing who will break the tie promotes open communication and encourages both partners to share their thoughts and feelings. This exchange fosters a deeper understanding of each other's perspectives. As I always say, "If you can't talk to each other, you can't build."

It establishes clarity.

When couples can agree on who will make the final decision, it provides clarity and eliminates confusion. This agreement creates a clear process for resolving disagreements and ensures that both partners understand their roles in decision-making.

It Prevents extended conflict.

Shelving unresolved issues doesn't work, they resurface again and again. Deciding who will break the tie avoids unnecessary conflicts by creating a pathway forward. This clarity reduces stagnation, allowing you and your partner to focus on your goals.

It builds trust.

Trust is a cornerstone of any strong relationship. Deciding who will break the tie reinforces trust and mutual respect. When approached with care, this practice strengthens the bond between partners, creating a solid foundation for the relationship.

Practical Applications of the "Who Breaks the Tie" Method

Finances

Major financial decisions, such as purchasing a home or setting a budget, often require a clear decision-maker. In these moments, deciding who breaks the tie can prevent arguments and ensure financial discussions are productive. This allows both partners to express their insights and concerns while allowing for resolution when a final decision has to be made.

Children

Parenting decisions, such as choosing schools or disciplinary methods, can also benefit from the "who breaks the tie" method. Partners can divide responsibilities based on their strengths, ensuring that decisions are made with expertise and care. For example, one partner may be more vital in school selection while the other is more versed in extra-curricular activities. Remember, one size doesn't fit all, just like the same partner may not always be the final decision-maker regarding the children. I always advise couples to lean into their strengths and enjoy the power of having someone they can lean on in areas where they are not as strong.

Deciding Where to Live

Choosing where to live, whether for a job opportunity or family needs, is another area where a clear decision-maker can help. Setting egos aside and prioritizing shared goals ensures that these decisions strengthen the relationship rather than create division.

Conclusion

"Who Breaks the Tie?" is a critical question in marriage. Having this conversation with your partner brings clarity and confidence when it comes to decision-making. Having the courage to explore this question requires commitment and intentionality. But believe me, it is worth the effort. There is no right or wrong method in answering this question, the most important thing is that you agree on how to approach decision making together. My advice is to use the reflections questions from this chapter and the workbook exercises to practice and apply this tool effectively.

REFLECTION QUESTIONS

1. Do you and your partner have clarity on how decisions are made in your relationship, especially when you disagree?

2. Are you leveraging each other's strengths to determine who is best suited to lead in different areas of your life?

3. What difference would it make in your relationship to have a structured process for handling decisions, reducing tension, and building trust?

4. Have you ever thought about how to approach major life decisions together in a way that builds confidence for both of you?

5. How would it transform your relationship to know you have a clear framework for navigating those tie-breaking moments together?

YOUR NEXT STEP ...

Decision-making can either bring you closer together or drive a wedge between you. These reflections help you see where you and your partner stand, but true alignment comes from having a clear process for navigating challenges. The workbook provides the framework you need to identify strengths, clarify roles, and resolve conflicts effectively. With these tools, you can confidently handle any decision, knowing you're working together, not against each other. Don't let unresolved disagreements linger; use the workbook to create a system that works for both of you.

Chapter 5
Do We Agree?

"Then God said, 'Let us make man in our image, after our likeness…'"
— Genesis 1:26

About a year ago, when I began writing this book, I came across Genesis 1:26 and noticed something I hadn't fully seen before: the word "us" in the first line. It wasn't as if I'd missed it in past readings, but this time, because my focus was studying relationships, I had a fresh perspective. Seeing the word "us" made me realize that we were created from a foundation of agreement. There was a plural element involved in our creation. If "us" did the making, then agreement was a requirement. The power of agreement is literally at the very core of our existence.

Let's take it a step further. Our bodies function best in agreement. In optimal health, every limb and cell works in concert with the others. When our bodies fail, it is often due to a foreign element introduced or disagreement within the body. Agreement is the glue that holds us together. If we're truly beings of agreement, then everything we're a part of operates best when grounded in unity. So consider this: marriage, an institution designed for us by "us", is at its strongest when rooted in agreement.

The context of marriage is two becoming one. Just as the body is made to operate within the context of agreement, so is marriage. This chapter will explore the final question of this book: "*Do we agree?*" The power of agreement cannot be underestimated in a relationship because it sets the tone for how couples navigate life together. Genesis 1:26 highlights the truth that we thrive in environments where agreement is the foundation.

When you say, "I do," you're really saying, "I agree." You're agreeing to everything you know about your partner and choosing to connect your life to theirs. You're saying, "I accept them as they are, including their strengths, any debts they may have, and their worldview. For everything I know about them, I choose to say, 'I agree'."

Ideally, this means both people are aligning on goals, values, vision, and roles. But I've found that, in many cases, there were never any in-depth conversations regarding these topics. Agreement wasn't established before saying, "I do." Neither partner checked to see if they were walking in agreement before committing to a lifelong partnership.

So, let's define and champion the necessity of agreement. It's about finding common ground and working together toward a shared future. And let's be clear, this doesn't mean you won't have disagreements. However, failing to align in the core areas of life sets you up for a guaranteed collision that could be avoided if this question was discussed.

This final section invites you to take an intentional journey of discovery to see if you and your partner are aligned in these key areas, clearing the path to deeper understanding and connection. I'll lay out a framework to help you understand the anatomy of agreement with your partner and to see if the two of you can genuinely agree.

The Requirements for Agreement

A Valid Agreement Requires Honesty

An agreement only works if both people are honest. Honesty must be at the core of any valid agreement. I can't tell you how many couples I've counseled who agreed to something verbally just to please their partner but had no intention of following through. Genuine agreement requires more than words; it demands integrity in action.

There are countless areas in a relationship where agreement is essential, from roles and responsibilities in the home to raising children and even the frequency of physical intimacy. Relationships fall apart when honesty is missing. If you or your partner struggle to be open because of fear about how it might impact the relationship, that's a red flag. If there's been a lack of honesty, now is the time to lay it all out before you take that next step into marriage.

The most critical advice I can give to couples considering marriage is to resist the pressure to tell your partner what they want to hear at the expense of the truth. Rarely do we admit the destructive nature of avoiding honesty. Whether it's discomfort with conflict or believing they can't handle the truth, avoiding honesty is deceit. And, deceit simply delays the inevitable destruction of the relationship.

. . .

Stephen Covey said it best: *"Trust is the glue of life. It's the most essential ingredient in effective communication. It's the foundational principle that holds all relationships."*[1] If you want a healthy marriage, you must choose to commit to telling the truth, plain and simple. That's the only way your agreements truly carry weight.

Take a moment to evaluate your relationship. Have you been completely honest with your partner? Reflect on your level of transparency. Are there any areas where you're holding back out of fear? If so, now is the time to start those conversations. You owe it to both of you.

A Valid Agreement Requires Clear Communication

Clear communication is not a given. Have you ever read one of those contracts on your phone and stopped to read a few lines before scrolling down to click "agree"? It's confusing. Sometimes, conversations between partners can feel the same way, a lot of words with no clear outcome. When it comes to agreement, the goal is to communicate clearly so your partner knows exactly where you stand.

. . .

For example, let's say you ask your partner, "Are we settled on me being the one to break the tie if we can't agree on a finance issue?" Instead of a straightforward response, they take a confusing detour, saying something like, "Well, when I was a child, my mother made a financial decision that almost ruined our family, so even though you know more about finances, I'm uncomfortable deciding that right now." Then they suggest waiting until a financial decision comes up to figure it out. By the end of the conversation, not only are you unsure where they stand, but you're also left with even less clarity than when the discussion began. You leave the conversation frustrated and stuck because they didn't give you a clear yes or no. Even if they had just said no, at least you'd know where they stood.

If clear communication is a struggle, try this: skip the backstory. Declutter your communication by going directly to a simple "yes" or "no," then create space for more conversation. Begin with clarity, and let everything else build from there. Will this make some conversations harder? Yes. But it will also make them far more meaningful. Too often, we use long backstories to soften the truth of how we really feel, then get frustrated when our partner doesn't comprehend the weight of what we're saying. When communication isn't clear, it leaves too much room for assumptions, and you can still leave the conversation feeling misunderstood and without clarity. I know we all love a good story, but when we lead with stories, instead of being clear about where we stand, we end up hiding our hearts behind the stories.

Clear communication is the foundation for genuine agreement. When you speak with clarity, agreement is possible. And when agreement is possible, you can thrive. So, let's look at the areas where agreement is critical.

Identifying the Necessary Areas of Agreement

Here are the key areas in a relationship where agreement can create a healthy, thriving partnership.

Intimacy

Can we agree when it comes to intimacy?

Intimacy is at the heart of any relationship. When couples openly discuss and agree on expectations for both physical and emotional intimacy, they deepen their connection. Honest conversations about each other's needs and desires are essential, covering topics like boundaries, preferences and frequency. Saying something like, "Physical intimacy is really important to me," but expecting your partner to know that means you want physical intimacy five times a week is unrealistic. Relationships built on assumptions or mind-reading remain surface-level. Speak up, express your desires clearly, and work together to align on what intimacy means for both of you.

. . .

A lifelong commitment means really understanding the role you've signed up for, and that includes being in tune with your partner's needs when it comes to intimacy. It's not about striving for perfection but about showing up as the person you committed to be, for, and with them. That starts with a clear understanding of who they are and a genuine commitment to honoring your agreement regarding their intimacy needs. Please remember that agreeing does not mean it has to make sense to you. You may not think what they need is necessary, but that is not for you to judge, nor does it mean you should attempt to talk them out of it. Honor their needs and decide whether or not you have the capacity to meet them at their points of need. Then, be honest about it. When you're both able to meet each other's needs for intimacy, you're building on a strong foundation of love and understanding that can lead to a truly powerful union. When you can come to an agreement around intimacy, you avoid the frustration of assumptions and unspoken expectations and build a more satisfying and fulfilling connection with each other.

Finances

Can we agree when it comes to finances?

Finances are another critical source of conflict in relationships. In fact, in my years of experience in counseling, finances and intimacy are "1" and "1a" (in no particular order) in the critical areas of conflict in a relationship. When couples agree on how they will manage their finances, they can avoid the many pitfalls of financial stress. Talk about savings, budgeting, and large purchases. The more you discuss finances, the fewer surprises you'll face after saying, "I do." Here are some questions that are worth exploring when taking the journey to a financial agreement.

Couples' Finance Questions:

- What are our financial goals, short-term and long-term?
- How much will we save each month?
- Will homeownership be a goal?
- Who is responsible for the household bills?
- Will financial contributions to the home be based on our income or some other criteria?
- What other big purchases could we be entertaining, and how will we pay for them?
- What about tuition (if there are kids), and is that a joint effort as well?

This list is detailed for a reason: the more you talk through the financial aspects of your relationship, the less room there is for assumptions or confusion. In marriage, surprises should be limited, especially when it comes to money. The fewer surprises, the greater your chances of building consistency and fostering growth together. That is why it is so important to talk about every aspect of your finances. Take the time to dig deep in this area.

The last thing you want is to get to the other side of "I do" and realize you are just now learning your partner's beliefs or habits about money. Even worse, you might find out about debt that was never discussed. Finances are far too important to the health of your relationship to leave unchecked. When it comes to money in marriage, you need to know exactly what you are agreeing to. By coming to an agreement about your current financial situation and creating a shared vision and strategy for the future, you will not only gain an accountability partner but also a deeper sense of trust. Make sure you are aligned when it comes to your finances because it is foundational to your journey together.

Decision-Making

Can we agree when it comes to decision-making?

One of the most important aspects of any marriage is how the two of you will make decisions together. Agreement in this area deserves your full attention. In Chapter 4, "Who Breaks the Tie," we discussed the importance of having a clear understanding of how decisions will be made as a couple. If something as simple as deciding where to eat can turn into a challenge, imagine how critical it is to get on the same page when it comes to major life decisions.

When you and your partner agree on a decision-making process, you can avoid the tug-of-war that often happens when decisions are left to the heat of the moment. Whether you lean on consensus, compromise, or delegation, the goal is to establish a plan ahead of time.

To get started, consider these questions:

• Should we let the person with the most knowledge or expertise in the area take the lead?
• Will the same person have the final say in all major decisions?
• Will we always make sure to talk things through before taking action on big decisions?

These questions can help create a healthy foundation for decision-making as a team. Agreeing on how you'll handle this before marriage gives you both peace of mind and sets the stage for a vision you'll carry forward after saying "I do." Having a clear strategy for navigating life's big choices is like having a compass—it keeps you on track. When you've already had these conversations, it's easier to recognize when you've veered off course and make the adjustments together.

. . .

Agreement is your roadmap when the path ahead feels unclear. Remember, God brought us into existence through a moment of divine agreement. That's why harmony and peace flow so naturally when agreement is present in our bodies and in our relationships. Asking the question, "Can we agree?" is powerful. It has the potential to shape the entire course of your marriage. That's how essential it is.

There will be seasons in your marriage where you'll need to revisit these conversations to ensure you're still aligned. Life changes, and so do we, but starting your marriage without clarity in these key areas creates unnecessary struggles. If disagreement becomes the norm, it can be tough to move forward. Before you take that step into marriage, make sure you and your partner are building on a foundation of real agreement. It's a decision that will serve you both for the rest of your lives.

Conclusion

At the end of the day, this is why I wrote this book. These questions and conversations are here to give you the confidence you need before stepping into a lifelong commitment. When you say "I do," you should have as much clarity as possible about what you're agreeing to.

Agreement is a powerful force in any marriage.Without it, stagnation, frustration, and lingering conflicts are inevitable. Marriage is about two becoming one, but when agreement is missing, it's as if that "one body" is at odds with itself, struggling to stay healthy. A commitment to agreement is what keeps that body (your marriage) strong. When two people align, they're able to work effectively together and pursue shared goals. By focusing on areas of agreement, embracing compromise, and communicating openly, couples build a solid foundation.

This entire book has been about laying everything out on the table and asking, 'Can we agree before we say I do?' Agreement is the glue that holds all other aspects together, "Can we agree on our vision, purpose, finances, and who breaks the tie?" Agreement is the framework for a marriage that thrives.

. . .

My prayer is that this book has given you a clearer understanding of what it truly means to prepare for marriage before you say, "I do." Use these insights to start building a strong, lasting relationship well before you pick out a ring or decide on a date. The goal is to engage your mind and develop the discipline needed in these key areas. Marriage is a beautiful and sacred union, but it requires intentional preparation. When you take the time to ask the right questions before marriage, you are setting yourselves up to pursue your highest vision and live out the dreams you have imagined together.

Remember:
"If you want to go fast, go alone. If you want to go far, go together."[2]

Don't worry, you got this. Keep loving each other and keep asking questions. The journey will unfold on a path of intentional conversations.

With Prayer and Love,
Ray Murray

REFLECTION QUESTIONS

1 How aligned are you and your partner on key areas like goals, finances, and intimacy?

2 Have you assessed where you're in sync and where there might be gaps?

3 Imagine creating a commitment statement reflecting your shared values and goals, how would that strengthen your relationship?

4 How would it feel to have a system to evaluate and strengthen your compatibility across critical areas?

YOUR NEXT STEP ...

Agreement is the foundation of a strong marriage, but getting there takes intentional effort. These reflections give you insight into where you align as a couple, but the workbook takes it further, helping you bridge the gaps and celebrate your strengths. Through guided exercises, you'll create a commitment statement that reflects your shared values and gives you a framework to revisit as your relationship evolves. Don't stop at reflection; use the workbook to solidify your agreement and set the stage for a partnership built on unity and understanding.

Notes

1. What's Your Vision?

1. Helen Keller Quote: The only thing worse than being blind is having sight but no vision. - Quoatable. https://www.quoatable.com/helen-keller-quote-the-only-thing-worse-than-being-blind-is-having-sight-but-no-vision/
2. *The Holy Bible, King James Version*. New York: American Bible Society, 1999. Proverbs 29:18.
3. American Legal Journal. "Divorce Rates Statistics and Trends for 2024." *American Legal Journal*. Accessed October 16, 2024. https://americanlegaljournal.com/divorce-statistics-trends-2024.
4. Vision Of Love – City News. https://www.citynews.sg/2011/07/11/vision-of-love/

2. Is Your Partner Compatible With Your Purpose?

1. Mark Twain, *The Wit and Wisdom of Mark Twain*, ed. Alex Ayres (New York: Harper & Row, 1987), 88.
2. David S. Viscott, *Finding Your Strength in Difficult Times: A Book of Meditations* (New York: McGraw-Hill, 1993), 118.

3. Can We Talk About Finances?

1. Thomas Jefferson, quoted in Henry Augustine Washington, ed., *The Writings of Thomas Jefferson* (Washington, D.C.: Taylor & Maury, 1853), 60.
2. Ramsey Solutions. "Money Fights Are the Second Leading Cause of Divorce." *Ramsey Solutions*, accessed October 16, 2024. https://www.ramseysolutions.com/relationships/money-fights-are-the-second-leading-cause-of-divorce.
3. MagnifyMoney. "One in Five Americans Admit to Financial Infidelity, Survey Finds." *MagnifyMoney*, accessed October 16, 2024. https://www.magnifymoney.com/blog/news/financial-infidelity-survey.

4. Ally Bank. "Ally Bank Survey Finds 70 Percent of Couples Argue About Money More Than Any Other Topic." *Ally Bank*, accessed October 16, 2024. https://www.ally.com/do-it-right/trends/money-and-relationships.

4. Who Breaks the Tie?

1. Anonymous, "In marriage, it's less about thinking alike and more about thinking together."
2. Simon Sinek, *Leaders Eat Last: Why Some Teams Pull Together and Others Don't* (New York: Portfolio/Penguin, 2014), 47.

5. Do We Agree?

1. Stephen R. Covey, *The 7 Habits of Highly Effective People: Powerful Lessons in Personal Change* (New York: Free Press, 1989), 203.
2. African proverb, attributed.

About the Author

Ray Murray is a man on a mission to help a generation seeking real answers. As someone who refuses to accept the phrase "that is just the way it is," he has dedicated his life to challenging the status quo and empowering people to live outside of the box with purpose, truth, and clarity.

With over a decade of counseling experience, Ray is a certified SYMBIS counselor, a trusted relationship and life coach, and the executive pastor at Hope's House Christian Ministries. Whether delivering spiritual messages from the pulpit, counseling couples preparing for marriage, or inspiring audiences on public stages, Ray embraces the intersection of culture and scripture with honesty, humor, and wisdom. His conversational approach has made him a sought-after voice for individuals and couples navigating the challenges of modern relationships both in business and personal spaces.

Ray holds a Bachelor of Science degree from the UC Berkeley Haas School of Business and two master's degrees, one in Christian Ministry and Counseling and another in Divinity, both from Liberty University School of Divinity. His blend of academic training and real-world experience uniquely equips him to guide others in personal growth and relational success.

At the heart of Ray's message is what he calls "correction, not perfection." As a recipient of God's unconditional love, he embraces his own journey of growth and uses it to inspire others to seek God's purpose for their lives. His passion for helping couples prepare for and strengthen their marriages is rooted in his belief that asking the right questions and having courageous conversations can transform relationships.

Ray is married to Vicki Murray, and together they navigate the joys and challenges of marriage and parenting in a blended family. Their children, Corey, Patrice, Julian, Jayden, and Kenedi, along with their grandson CJ, provide them with endless stories, laughter, and life lessons.

Through his work, Ray continues to equip individuals and couples to build lives and relationships on a foundation of purpose, understanding, and partnership.

TAKING THE NEXT STEP

Congratulations on taking this bold and necessary step. You didn't just read a book, you made an investment in the kind of marriage that doesn't just survive, but thrives with clarity, purpose, and real love.

But don't stop here.

Now that you've wrestled with the questions, it's time to walk through them. How? With your partner, with intentionality, and with a guide.

That's why I created the Before You Get Married 5-Day Challenge.

This isn't just a recap. It's a deeper dive. Five days. Five powerful questions. And I'll walk you through each one personally. You'll get to unpack what you've read, reflect on what it means for your relationship, and apply tools that go far beyond theory. This is where things get real.

The challenge is self-paced, but fully guided. You'll watch me teach, coach, and walk through the same tools I've used for over a decade in premarital counseling with exercises and assignments designed to spark life-changing conversations between you and your partner.

If the book helped you think it through, this challenge helps you live it out.
- ☑ Define your shared vision
- ☑ Clarify your purpose as individuals and as a couple
- ☑ Create a real-time financial plan
- ☑ Establish your tie-breaker strategy
- ☑ Confirm if you both agree before you say "I do"

Don't just talk about having a strong foundation. Build one.

For access to the challenge and other resources:
- Visit BeforeUGetMarried.com
- Follow me on Instagram: @iamraymurray
- Or tap in at iamraymurray.com

I'm proud of you. I'm praying for you. And I'm walking with you.

With purpose and love,

Ray Murray

www.ingramcontent.com/pod-product-compliance
Lightning Source LLC
Chambersburg PA
CBHW052141270326
41930CB00012B/2980